This book belongs to

This book is dedicated to anyone who may be having a bad day - child or adult. May you find the strength to process your emotions in a healthy way and turn your day around. The sun always shines again.

To my support system: I love you all.

Jonah's Bad Day
Copyright ©2025 by Demira Hymes. All Rights Reserved. Published by Beyond Blessed Publishing

All rights reserved. No part of this publication may be reproduced, distributed, or transmitted in any form or by any means, including photocopying, recording, or other electronic or mechanical methods, without the prior written permission of the publisher, except in the case of brief quotations embodied in critical reviews and certain other noncommercial uses permitted by copyright law. For permission requests, write to the publisher, addressed "Attention: Permissions Coordinator," at the email below.

beyondblessedpublishing@gmail.com
Title: Jonah's Bad Day/Demira Hymes
Identifiers: ISBN: 979-8-9994490-0-9 (hardcover)

Any references to historical events, real people, or real places are used fictitiously.
Names, characters, and places are products of the author's Imagination.

Published and Printed in the USA
First Printing Edition 2025.
Publisher: Beyond Blessed Publishing

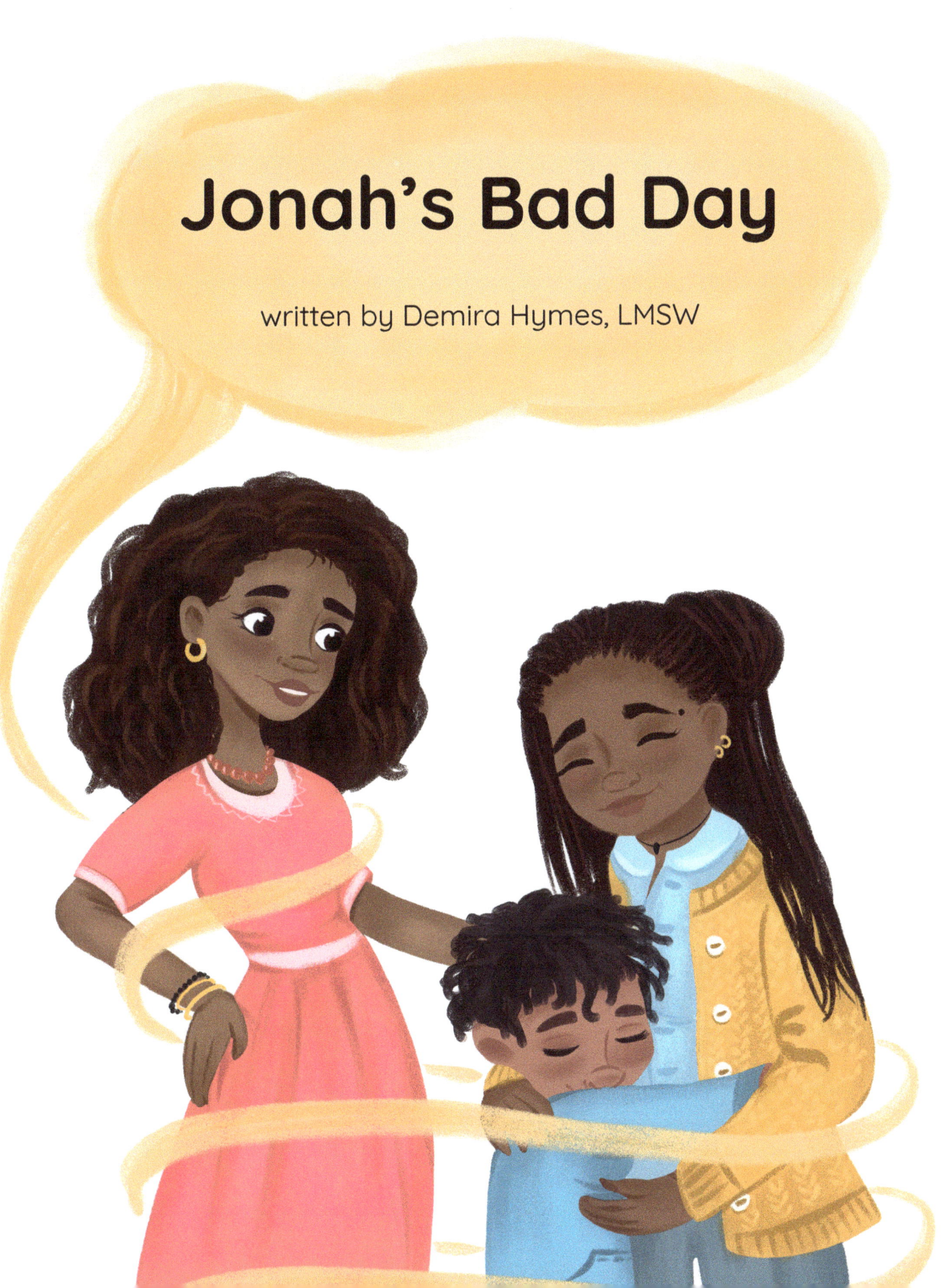

Jonah woke up late for school today.

An unusual event in his daily routine. He tossed and turned all night but just couldn't sleep right.

When he got out of bed and looked out the window, he saw it was raining outside. Jonah sighed, he hated when it rained.
The gloomy weather made him feel all yucky inside, he didn't like going out in the rain.

"Jonah, get ready for school! You're already late!" Jonah's mama yelled as she entered his room with her hand on her hip.

Jonah turned from his window and looked at her with a frown on his face, he hated being yelled at.

"But mama, it's raining outside.
I don't want to go to school."
He retorted with a face full of sadness.

"I don't have time to talk about it, Jonah. You're going to school, so we have to get moving. We'll talk about it later, okay?" She spoke softly before quickly leaving his room.

Jonah wiped away the tears that fell from his eyes ...

as he began to get dressed.

His mama had hurt his feelings, and that made him feel sad.

At school, Jonah was not in a good mood. He sat at his desk with his arms folded across his chest. His teacher asked him questions, but he ignored her and put his head on his desk.

He felt a mixture of emotions that he did not know how to express. He was tired, sad, and irritated, and to top it all off, he had a spelling test.
Jonah knew he wouldn't be able to do his best, so he kept his head down and slept through the test.

Next, it was lunch time, and Jonah sat by himself in the cafeteria; he did not want to be bothered. His mama didn't have time to pack his lunch like usual, so he had to eat school lunch.

Jonah sighed heavily as he stared blankly at his lunch tray; it consisted of meat loaf, mashed potatoes and peas. Jonah didn't like any of the food on his tray, so he pushed it away before pulling his hoodie over his head and putting his head down on the table.

At recess, it was still raining out, so everyone had to stay inside. Jonah's friends Naomi and Micah asked to play board games with him, but he declined.

He wanted to be left alone so he went and sat in the corner of the classroom and watched his classmates play. Jonah's chest felt tight; today just wasn't his day.

"Jonah, what's wrong?" His teacher queried, approaching him with worry on her face, "You don't seem like yourself today; you didn't even take your spelling test."

Jonah didn't know how to express the way he was feeling, so he simply said, "Leave me alone."

His teacher looked at him, surprised at his response. She knew Jonah very well, and the behavior he was showing did not seem like him at all. She knew something was off and that she would need more assistance to handle the situation. She went to her desk to make a phone call.

Soon, recess was over, and everyone was back at their desks, getting ready for their next lesson. There was a sudden knock at the classroom door, which grabbed everyone's attention.

Ms. Brown went to answer it, and Jonah watched as she spoke to someone outside the classroom door. At this point, he was ready to go home because he was beginning to feel bored.

"Jonah, come here." Ms. Brown said gently from the door. He looked at her in confusion but got up from his desk and met her at the classroom door.

"Do you remember Ms. Walker?" Ms. Brown questioned him.

Jonah looked at Ms. Walker and for the first time today, he smiled. Ms. Walker was the nice lady who always asked students how they were feeling, would play games with them, and had good snacks in her office.

"Yes" he answered as he looked back at his teacher.

"Well, she came by to pull you out of class for a few minutes, is that okay?"

Jonah nodded his head yes.

"How about we take a trip to my office?" Jonah nodded his head yet again and followed her lead.

As they walked through the hallway, Jonah wondered why Ms. Walker was pulling him out of class. Was he in trouble? Now, he was beginning to feel anxious.

Once they got to her office, Jonah immediately picked up one ...

of the many fidget spinners she had in a bucket on a table and started playing with it.

"Would you like a snack?" Ms. Walker asked as she sat at her desk. Jonah was hungry so, he immediately answered, "Yes."

Ms. Walker pointed to her snack box and allowed Jonah to pick out a snack. After settling on a bag of chips, Jonah sat down on the light blue bean bag in the corner of her office.

"Do you remember what I do here?"
Ms. Walker asked him.

Jonah nodded his head before answering, "Yes, you ask kids how they're feeling and give out good snacks."
Ms. Walker chuckled at his response.

"That's somewhat true. I'm the social worker here, so I do a lot of different things, but my main job is to help students and families in need. That starts with checking in on you guys and seeing how you're feeling." Ms. Walker explained.

Jonah nodded his head as he listened intently.

"So, how are you today?" Ms. Walker asked
"I'm not feeling good today." He expressed.
"Why not?" Ms. Walker looked at him.

Jonah looked down at his hands and shrugged his shoulders before telling Ms. Walker all the bad things that had happened so far in the day.

"I'm just having a bad day, and my feelings are all over the place." He concluded.

Jonah finally looked up at Ms. Walker to see that she was looking back at him and was listening to every word he said. He felt heard, like his voice and feelings mattered.

"It sounds like your day was off to a rough start. I'm sorry your mom yelled at you Jonah. I'm sure she didn't mean it; sometimes, adults get frustrated and may process those feelings the wrong way. I also can understand you not wanting to be at school because of the rain, but the good thing is the rain won't last forever". Ms. Walker smiled.

Jonah nodded his head and relaxed his shoulders; he was beginning to feel calmer and less upset.

"It's okay to feel sad, angry, or upset, Jonah. Even though you're young, you are still human, and we all have feelings and emotions."
Ms. Walker continued, "When you're feeling overwhelmed with emotions, it's good to do breathing exercises. Like this..."

Jonah watched as Ms. Walker breathed through her nose before doing the same thing.
"Now breathe out through your mouth." She instructed before blowing out through her mouth.

Jonah followed her movements and breathed out through his mouth. For the first time that day, he felt relaxed.

"How do you feel?" Ms. Walker asked softly with a cute smile.
"Good, I feel calmer. Like a big weight was lifted off my shoulders." Jonah explained.
"That's what I love to hear. Breathing exercises can help regulate your emotions and make you feel better. I even like to do breathing exercises when I'm having a rough moment. So, when you're upset, sad, or angry, try taking some deep breaths to calm yourself down." Ms. Walker suggested.
"Okay, I can do that." Jonah nodded.

"You can also request to come talk to me or another trusted adult. You might want to take a few minutes to yourself just to regroup or go on a walk to process your feelings. I want you to remember that a few bad moments don't have to lead to a bad day." She stated warmly.

"It doesn't?" Jonah inquired. He thought for sure his whole day was ruined.

Ms. Walker smiled. "Nope. For example, it's only 1 o'clock right now. You still have the rest of the day to have a good day. I know you had a rough morning, but you can have a good afternoon. I think it even stopped raining outside."

Jonah stood up and walked to the window.
The rain had indeed stopped, and now the sun was beaming softly like a newborn baby. His eyes brightened.

"It did stop!" He announced excitedly with a smile while looking back at Ms. Walker.

"See, bad moments don't last forever, so it's okay to feel like you're having a bad day, but the bad feelings do not have to stay. They should disappear fast, like morning dew.

You've got this. Remember the breathing techniques we did and other things you can do to manage your emotions, like journaling, coloring, or drawing. This can help turn a bad day into a good one." She encouraged him.

Jonah smiled, "Thank you so much, Ms. Walker." He walked to her desk and hugged her.

"I feel so much better being able to talk about my feelings, and you helped me learn how to manage them. It didn't feel good holding them in. Will you come by Ms. Brown's classroom tomorrow and get me?" He looks at her quizzically.

"Of course, Jonah, I'll continue to check in on you if you'd like. Are you ready to go back to class?"
She asked with a smile.

Jonah took a deep breath and smiled, **"Yes, I'm ready to have a good day"**!

He walked out of Ms. Walker's office ready to take on the rest of the day. Jonah went back to class and kept his head up throughout the rest of the lessons, his teacher even let him retake his spelling test.

Since it stopped raining, they were able to go outside, and Jonah played tag with his friends Naomi and Micah.
He was having so much fun that he managed to forget that he had a bad morning.

When Jonah got home, his mom had his favorite snack apples and peanut butter, waiting on him at the kitchen table.
How was school?" she asked him before kissing his forehead.

Jonah sat down at the kitchen table and began eating his snack. "It started out rough, but it got better."

His mom sighed, "I apologize for yelling at you this morning, and I'm sorry if that negatively affected your day. We woke up late, and I was all over the place this morning. That still didn't give me a reason to hurt your feelings."

"It's okay mama, I forgive you. Next time, try breathing in through your nose and out through your mouth to help calm you down. It really worked for me today, so it might work for you." Jonah replied reassuringly.

His mama laughed, "I will try that. You are so smart. Come give me a hug."

He granted his mama's request and gave her a big hug. "I love you," she said as she kissed the top of his head.

"I love you too." He smiled. As he enjoyed his mama's warm embrace, Jonah thought to himself, maybe his day wasn't so bad after all.

www.ingramcontent.com/pod-product-compliance
Lightning Source LLC
Chambersburg PA
CBHW051327110526
44582CB00003B/77